D0906487

Basics of
Investing

By Marc Robinson

TIME LIFE BOOKS ®

Alexandria, Virginia

State Street Global Advisors: educating people about money

For 200 years, we have been in the banking business helping people manage and invest their money. We are a global leader in the investment management industry, serving institutions and individuals worldwide.

Our goal in creating this series is to give you unbiased, useful information that will help you manage your money. No product advertisements. No sales pitches. Just straightforward, understandable information.

Our ultimate hope is that after reading these books you feel more informed, more in control of your money, and perhaps most importantly, more able to successfully plan and reach your financial goals.

Time-Life Books is a division of
TIME LIFE INCORPORATED

Time-Life Custom Publishing
Vice President and Publisher: Terry Newell
Director of Sales: Neil Levin
Director, New Business Development: Phyllis A. Gardner
Senior Art Director: Christopher M. Register
Managing Editor: Donia Ann Steele
Production Manager: Carolyn Bounds
Quality Assurance Manager: James D. King

© 1996 Top Down

All rights reserved. No part of this book may be reproduced in any form or by any electronic or mechanical means, including information storage and retrieval devices or systems, without prior written permission from the publisher, except that brief passages may be quoted for reviews.

First Printing. PRINTED IN U.S.A.

Time Life is a registered trademark of Time Warner Inc. U.S.A.

Books produced by Time-Life Custom Publishing are available at special bulk discount for promotional and premium use. Custom adaptations can also be created to meet your specific marketing goals.

Call 1-800-323-5255

For State Street Global Advisors, The Lab:
Clark Kellogg
Jenny Phillips
Sally Nellson
Paul Schwartz

For Top Down:
Marc Robinson
Mark Shepherd
Research: Richard Kroll

The information contained in this publication is general in nature and is not intended to provide advice, guidance, or expertise of any nature regarding financial or investment decisions. Neither Time-Life Books, State Street Bank and Trust Company, Marc Robinson, or Top Down make any representations or warranties with respect to the professional experience or credentials of the authors or contributors, or to the merits of the information of materials contained herein. The reader should consult independent financial advisors and investment professionals prior to making any decision or plan.

Robinson, Marc, 1955-
    Basics of Investing : it's just what you need to know / by Marc
  Robinson
        p. cm. -- (Time Life Books your money matters)
      ISBN 0-7835-4792-7
      1. Investments. 2. Finance, Personal. I. Title. II. Series.
HG4521. R664 1996
332.6--dc20   95-50116
                                  CIP

ABLE OF Contents

The big picture:
You're in control of your mone

If you have money—even a paycheck—you have to use it somehow. And with every decision comes a risk: You always have something to gain and lose—even if you do nothing. Whether you're the type who can't let go of money, who at least needs to keep a close eye on it, or one who can easily trust someone else with it, the question you have to ask yourself is: How are you going to use it?

➌ Store it at a **bank**

Banks want to borrow your money. By opening an account, you lend it to them until you need it. In return, you may get a
- checking account for convenient, quick access to your cash;
- savings or money market account, where the bank continuously lends your money for short periods, collects a small fee (interest) each time, and splits the profits with you; o
- certificate of deposit (CD), where you lend money for a specific period of time at a fixed rate of interest.

➋ Save it and keep it **at home**

You may feel secure stashing money at home—you know where it is, it's available any time, and you won't lose it. But this is actually a sure way to lose money because inflation will slowly erode its buying power. Your job is to find a way to fight against that.

➊ Spend it
yourself

The crowd favorite.

❹ Buy publicly owned companies

You could become a part-owner of companies by buying shares of their stock. If the companies do well, you could participate in the success. If they do poorly, you may lose money, just like any company owner would.

❺ Lend to businesses and governments

You could lend money by buying bonds or other fixed income securities (in which the borrower repays lenders like you in steady, fixed amounts, providing them with income). Government entities and companies borrow money for many reasons, such as to make repairs or improvements, or simply to have more money to operate. You'll earn interest for letting someone else use your money.

❻ Pay a mutual fund
to lend or buy for you

Mutual funds are professional money managers for the masses. You decide on an objective (protection, income, growth, or a combination) then select one of the many funds that aims to achieve that objective. The profits and losses are yours, minus management or other fees.

❼ Buy real estate

You could buy a home or a piece of commercial real estate, such as an office building, shopping center, or even raw land. You gain or lose according to how the property value fluctuates.

❽ Gamble

You could just roll the dice, buy lottery tickets, or play any other game of chance and hope to make a profit—but also risk losing everything.

What's the reward?

Being a successful investor doesn't necessarily mean making a lot of money. Like choosing the proper attire for the weather, the way to think about reward is to choose a strategy and investments that fit your goal. And reward is the same for everybody: Whether you're rich or poor, a beginner or an expert,

there are only *three objectives* you can have:

Protect what you have

One objective is simply to keep what you already have saved. Even then, your money must earn more money. Otherwise, inflation will erode your buying power and leave you with less than when you started.

Safety is the top priority. That often means lending your money for short periods to borrowers with reliable reputations. Since borrowers can't do much with your money in short spans, they won't pay you much interest. But that's the trade-off. You keep your money close and safe, earning only enough interest to offset inflation and protect what you have.

Common investments for protection are:

- Savings accounts. Federally insured, open-ended loans to your bank.

- Certificates of deposit (CDs). Loans to your bank for specified periods.

- U.S. Treasury bills. Loans to the U.S. government for specified periods.

- Bank money market funds. FDIC-insured collections of short-term loans.

- Money market mutual funds. Uninsured collections of short-term loans.

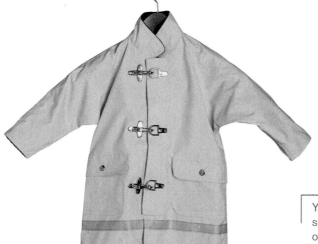

Mix and match

You don't have to be a purist. Many people split their money to accomplish several objectives. Many others find investments that blend objectives, such as protection and income or growth and income.

Liquidity

Many people want to keep money within quick, easy reach, so they put it in "liquid" investments. "Liquidity" is the ability to convert your money quickly into cash. Some investments can be converted more quickly than others.

For example, you can convert your savings account instantly into cash at any ATM; but it usually takes three days to sell stock and have the cash available. Real estate is one of the least liquid investments. There's no telling when you'll be able to sell it and receive the cash.

Earn income

You could give your money to someone who will promise to provide a regular, predictable income stream that may outpace inflation.

To earn income, people generally give up a little more control than when investing for protection: They lend money for longer periods but expect to be compensated more for it. For example, if you look at Treasury bond rates in the newspaper, you should see higher interest being offered for longer-term Treasuries. This is because the government will pay more interest in exchange for the extra time they can use your money.

Another way to earn income is to buy stock that pays a dividend (a quarterly profit distribution to the shareholders).

Some investments appropriate for income are:

Municipal bonds and U.S. Treasuries. Usually pay interest that's free from some income tax.

Corporate bonds. Usually pay interest that's taxable as income.

Utility stocks. Pay dividends quarterly.

Fixed income mutual funds. Pay income regularly, sometimes monthly.

Grow more

In the financial world, when people refer to growth they typically mean investments that appreciate in value.

Generally, stocks are investments for people whose goal is growth. Some stocks are even called "growth stocks," which tend to be shares of small companies that may be growing faster than the general stock market.

What's the risk?

Even outlandish clothes can be appropriate for a certain function. It's no different with investments. The risk is in using them for the wrong purposes. For example, you might think stocks are riskier than a savings account, and if you'll need every penny next week, it *would* be riskier because the price could drop. But if you're trying to raise money for college in 10 years, the slow-growing savings account would actually be riskier—because it will never earn you enough, while the stock someday might. In other words,

it's not the investment itself that's risky;
it's how you choose to use it.

You can't avoid it...

The moment you have money—even a paycheck—you have risk. You could literally lose the money. Prices could go up while you hold it, making what you want unaffordable. Even when you do nothing with money, you take risks: for example, not having enough money when you need it.

You have to take the risk that's *appropriate* for reaching your goal. If your goal is modest, you can take modest risks. If your goal is more challenging, you'll face greater risks— but you may also find ways to neutralize some of them.

...but you can weigh it

You always weigh risks with your money, finding the right balance and making choices accordingly. To buy or wait for a better deal. To save or spend. Even to carry a little or a lot in your wallet.

To find the proper balance, you have to weigh the risks of an investment against the risk of not reaching your goal (the reward). Without a goal, you can only assess a risk by your feelings.

The common perspective:	Another perspective:
"The greater the risk, the greater the potential for reward." This implies that the more risk you take the more money you can make.	You can easily increase your risk without adding the potential for more reward. So why do it, unless you won't reach your goal without it?
The common perspective: Certain types of investments are riskier than others (e.g., commodity futures are riskier than savings accounts, and stocks are riskier than bonds).	Another perspective: It's how you use it. For example, farmers use futures as insurance policies. To them, futures eliminate risk. As for bonds, many can be even more susceptible to losing value than the stocks of Fortune 500 companies.

A party

A business meeting

A funeral

...and you can control it

Just because you invest money somewhere—you let someone else use it—doesn't mean you've lost control. In fact, the financial world is designed specifically to help people control their risks while letting go of their money. It's a heavily "regulated" world, where new strategies are constantly being created in hopes of lowering risk without harming the potential for profit. As a beginner, you'll use a limited number of strategies to regulate how fast and far to go in reaching your goals. Advanced investors, though, often combine different kinds of investments in attempts to fine-tune their risks.

...and use it to your advantage

Risk is an essential tool of investing that you can use to your advantage. For example, you could invest in a very safe bond that pays low interest, or in a bond that's slightly less safe but pays more interest. If, historically, that level of increased risk hasn't caused problems, you may opt to earn the extra interest.

Conservative/aggressive ?
A strategy that's pitched as conservative may be very risky—for your goals. And an aggressive strategy may be your only sensible choice. It all depends on your goal.

Inflation and the real rate of return

As soon as you have money, you should understand inflation: How it affects you and how to protect yourself from it. Inflation refers to price increases: prices "inflate." But a better word might be "erosion," because money is a perishable item. Milk sours. Fruit rots. Money erodes—at a rate equal to the inflation rate. For example, if you hold onto $100 today to buy $100 of groceries and prices inflate 3% this year, you'll need $103 to buy those groceries a year from today (3% of your money will have eroded). If you don't pay attention to inflation, you'll never notice how much of your money disappears every year, as if the **money simply turns to dust that blows away into nothing n**

Finding the inflation rate

Inflation is commonly measured by the Consumer Price Index (CPI), which measures changes in your day-to-day expenses. The CPI is released in the middle of every month and published in most major newspapers. You can call a 24-hour recorded message on the CPI at (202) 606-STAT.

The **real rate** of return

It's important to know how much your money is earning. But to understand what you'll eventually end up with, it's just as important to know how much it is losing.

This is what's easy to see:
The interest you're earning from an investment.

This is what's not so easy to see:
The interest you're losing to inflation.

This is what's really important:
What remains is what you're really earning, called the "real rate of return." In this case, your 6.25% actually gives you only 3.65% after accounting for inflation.

Here's what many investment firms will tell you has happened to a $1 investment from 1926...

	...to 1994
Small company stocks	$2,842.77
Large company stocks	810.54
Long-term government bonds	25.86
U.S. Treasury bills	12.19
Inflation	8.35

Based on the Standard & Poor's 500 Stock Composite Index. Source: ©*Stocks, Bonds, Bills and Inflation Yearbook*,™ Ibbotson Associates, Chicago (annual update work by Roger G. Ibbotson and Rex A. Sinquefield). Used with permission. All rights reserved.

What causes inflation?

It isn't easy to determine, but here are two possible causes:

Too much money in circulation, indicated by either dropping unemployment figures (too many people with spending money) or increased government printing of money (money is too easy to get).

Not enough products being made to meet demand, indicated by either factories producing at near capacity or increased "housing starts" (too much demand for copper, wood, and other home building products). With increased demand, prices rise, and the same amount of money buys less.

The role of time

Everything changes over time—which makes time a critical part of every decision you make about what to do with your money. Whether you buy or sell, lend or borrow, time is a double-edged sword to be used thoughtfully, because

it can create **greater risks** *or* **greater rewards.**

It depends on how you use it

Time, like every other variable in investing, can be managed to fit your needs.

Allowing only short-term use. The sooner your money will be returned to you, the fewer chances exist for something to go wrong. So, if you only let go of your money for short stretches, you lessen time's risks.

On the other hand, you won't earn as much. The less time someone has with your money, the fewer things they can do with it—and, therefore, the less they'll be willing to pay you for the privilege of using it.

Allowing longer-term use. The more time remaining until your money is returned to you, the more chances for something to go wrong. So, if you let go of your money for long stretches, you lose more control and subject yourself to more of time's risks.

On the other hand, you can earn more because the more time borrowers have with your money, the more they can do with it. In return, they may be willing to pay you a larger fee for the use.

imagine a world in which you're paid to park–and the longer you park your money, the more you could be paid.

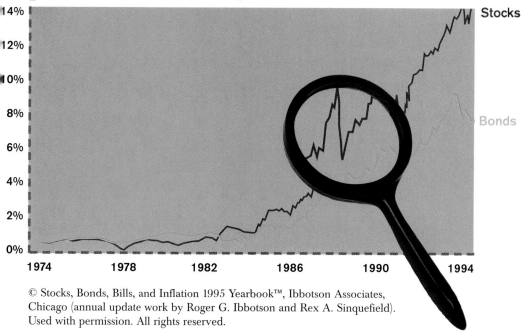

[Yearly return of stocks and bonds]

Stocks

Bonds

14% · 12% · 10% · 8% · 6% · 4% · 2% · 0%

1974 · 1978 · 1982 · 1986 · 1990 · 1994

© Stocks, Bonds, Bills, and Inflation 1995 Yearbook™, Ibbotson Associates, Chicago (annual update work by Roger G. Ibbotson and Rex A. Sinquefield). Used with permission. All rights reserved.

Your perspective

Having a goal—being able to look ahead to a certain point—gives you a big advantage when considering the risks of time. Without a goal, for instance, how can you know what's "too long," or what's "not long enough," other than by having a gut feeling? When you know how much time you have, your perspective on potential problems changes, as the chart above shows.

For example, the portion of the chart that's magnified includes the "Crash of 1987," the worst day in the history of the stock market (a 508-point, one-day drop). While it caused widespread, instant panic, look at how the market has performed since that time.

Short-term

If you have short-term objectives, short-term jumps and drops can look uncomfortably volatile to you. After all, you're running the risk of taking out your money at a loss simply because of your timing.

Long-term

If you have a long-term objective, you can take a broader, calmer, more studied view of the circumstances. From the perspective at this distance, all those dips merely seem part of a trend that's "up."

How time has historically reduced the risk of investing in stocks

The worst one-year performance of large-company stocks since 1926 was -43%. The worst five-year performance was -12%. Over 10 years it was only -1%. And the worst performance for 20 years was actually a gain of 3%.

Based on the Standard & Poor's 500 Stock Composite Index. Source: ©Stocks, Bonds, Bills and Inflation Yearbook,™ Ibbotson Associates, Chicago (annual update work by Roger G. Ibbotson and Rex A. Sinquefield). Used with permission. All rights reserved.

Two simple ways to grow money

When your money earns more money, it's natural to want to take that profit and use it—unless you want your money to grow. As money accumulates, it grows faster and faster—a powerful phenomenon known as "compound growth." Here are two strategies based on the idea of

keeping everyone's { **hands off** } *your money.*

1. Keep your hands off

It takes discipline to reinvest your earnings instead of spending them. But after a few years, the strategy really begins to pay off. The more your money accumulates, the faster your earnings accelerate.

Hands off. You start, for example, by investing $1,200 a year in a mutual fund that earns 8% a year. Every year, you reinvest your earnings so that they also earn 8% interest. After 20 years, you have almost $46,000 in savings after taxes (assuming a 28% marginal income tax bracket).

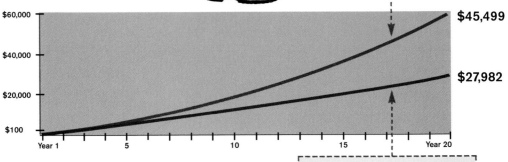

$45,499

$27,982

$60,000
$40,000
$20,000
$100
Year 1 — 5 — 10 — 15 — Year 20

Hands on. Every year, you earn the same 8%, but you only reinvest 2% of the earnings. After 20 years, you're left with almost $18,000 less.

It's automatic
Financial firms are happy to keep your money invested, so they often make it easy with automatic reinvestment plans.

Hands off. You invest $1,200 a year in a tax-free bond fund that earns 8% a year. Every year, you reinvest the earnings so that they also earn 8% interest. After 20 years, your money has grown to $59,308.

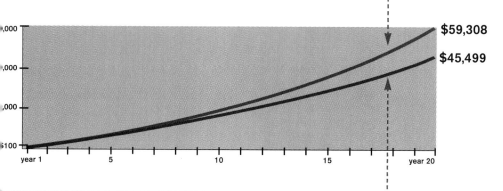

$59,308

$45,499

| year 1 | 5 | 10 | 15 | year 20 |

2. Keep the government's hands off

A major part of any plan to grow money involves avoiding paying taxes—legally. In fact, local, state, and federal governments encourage you to use your money in certain socially desirable ways by permitting you to skip paying taxes. For example, if you buy your state's municipal bonds (lend money to your state or local government), you won't pay federal income tax on the earnings. If you lend money to the federal government (buy Treasuries), you won't pay state and local income tax, although the federal government will still want its share of your earnings.

Reinvesting earnings makes your money grow at an accelerated pace. And if you can reinvest *all* your earnings—in other words, avoid taxes—you'll accelerate growth even more.

Hands on. You invest the same $1,200 and earn the same 8%, but every year you pay a 28% tax on earnings. After 20 years, you end up with nearly $14,000 less.

More hands-off ways
Retirement accounts, like an IRA or your company's 401(k), force you to keep your hands off and reward you for saving by keeping the government's hands off, too. All the money you earn in these accounts grows untaxed until you take it out for good. (Your contributions may not be taxed either.) That's why they're called "tax deferred plans." The tax payments are put off (deferred) until later, so your money has a chance to grow more quickly.

Buying and selling

These are the two most basic building blocks of investing. And they are governed by the simplest rule: Buy low and sell high. It's a simple thought but complicated in practice.

There are *two ways* to do it.

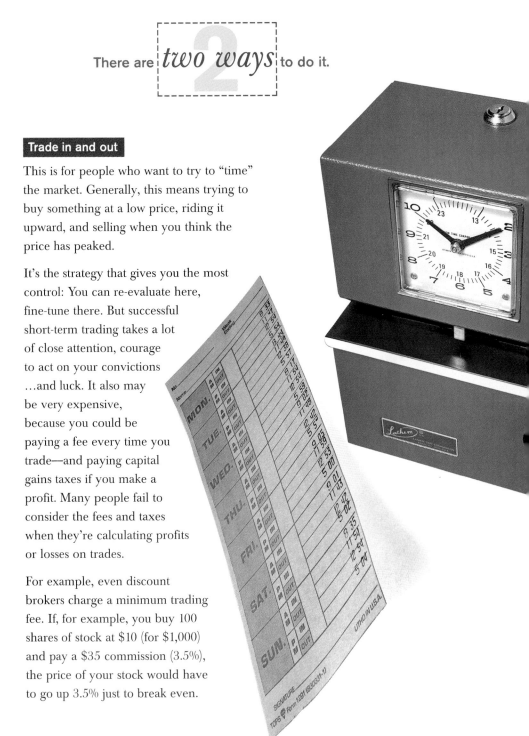

Trade in and out

This is for people who want to try to "time" the market. Generally, this means trying to buy something at a low price, riding it upward, and selling when you think the price has peaked.

It's the strategy that gives you the most control: You can re-evaluate here, fine-tune there. But successful short-term trading takes a lot of close attention, courage to act on your convictions …and luck. It also may be very expensive, because you could be paying a fee every time you trade—and paying capital gains taxes if you make a profit. Many people fail to consider the fees and taxes when they're calculating profits or losses on trades.

For example, even discount brokers charge a minimum trading fee. If, for example, you buy 100 shares of stock at $10 (for $1,000) and pay a $35 commission (3.5%), the price of your stock would have to go up 3.5% just to break even.

Buy and hold

f you take a longer-term approach—if your goals are more far-reaching—there's no pressing need to buy and sell quickly. You can find a use for your money that coincides with your goals, then give it time to do what you expect it to do. This is the strategy most financial professionals recommend, particularly for people who want their money to grow over time.

What's a "lot"?

Stocks are normally traded in blocks, or "round lots," of 100 shares. Because many stocks are high-priced, some people decide to buy fewer than 100—sometimes even two or three shares—to fit their budget. But buying in these "odd lots" is often an expensive strategy: Your order is filled after the orders from people buying in lots of 100 shares. You also have to wait for a seller who's willing to break up a round lot. You can expect any seller to charge a premium for breaking up a lot (because the leftovers from your sale will leave another odd lot to be sold).

[What prices do you pay?]

When you buy or sell stock, you can wait for a specific price, or you can buy or sell "at the market" (the current market price). The market price, however, is always different for buyers than it is for sellers. Here's how it works:

The market for a stock is listed according to its "bid" and "ask" price. When you buy, you pay the higher "ask"; if you immediately sold at the same market price, you'd be paid the lower "bid" price. The amount you'd automatically lose—the difference between the bid and ask—is called the "spread," the fee for the middlemen.

For example, say the bid on a stock is $20 and the ask is $20.50. If you buy, you'll pay $20.50; if you sell, you'll only receive $20. (In addition, you'll pay a broker's commission.)

Dollar cost averaging

This is a good strategy for real beginners with a resistance to using their money in ways they don't fully understand. It's also good for people who can afford to invest only small amounts of money at a time. This systematic, objective approach

is a way to fight *uncertainty* **over when to invest.**

It removes the guesswork

To implement this strategy, you choose:

- a certain stock, bond, or mutual fund as your target;
- a strict, regular schedule to invest;
- the amount of money to invest every time.

It doesn't take much money

The point is to accumulate a lot of shares over time without using a lot of money each time. Since you're not investing all at once, you don't need to have much—or anything—in savings in order to begin. You may even be able to force yourself to stick to the plan by having the money come directly from your paycheck or checking account each time.

It's methodical

Once you begin, you stick with the plan—no matter what happens to the price. Sometimes your money buys more, sometimes it buys less. At any time, you can total all your purchases and come up with your average cost. Then compare it to the current price of your investment. Anything above your cost is profit.

[It helps everyone]

Financial firms like this strategy because it's a relatively safe way to convince new clients to invest and keep investing. Of course, that's how these firms make money. But it's also good for clients. Most people need to learn how to save money and how it can continually earn more money for them.

There's good news and bad news

If the price goes down, your money will buy more shares. That's turning a disadvantage into an advantage, a fact that can neutralize the emotional letdown of seeing the price drop. If the price goes up, however, it's just the opposite. Some of the advantage of seeing your investment go up in price is taken away by having to pay more per share and receive fewer shares on new purchases.

Over time, it averages out

Total all the purchase prices and divide that amount by the number of shares you own. That's your average purchase price. Each time you buy, that average price will ratchet up or down somewhat, with the effect of keeping you on a more even keel. You may not make as much as you could have by investing all at once—but you may not lose as much, either.

What's your psychology?

If you're buying as the price goes down, will you be the kind of investor who wonders whether you're throwing good money after bad on a "dog" of a choice? Or will you trust that the price will rise eventually, and consider yourself lucky to have a chance to buy at "bargain" prices?

Diversification

How do you pick the right investments for the right times? Beginners and professionals alike u a simple strategy called "diversification." It involves spreading your money among a variety of investments that tend to react differently to different events. In a way, it's a catch-all strategy th

fights *uncertainty* over **what** to invest in

Finding a proper balance

If you invest too heavily in one area, you create a dangerous imbalance. One wrong set of circumstances could cause considerable losses. The chart at right shows how diversifying works: This hypothetical mix of winning and losing stocks, bonds, and other investments averages out to a 4.8% return.

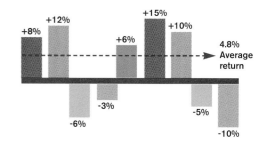

+8% +12% +15% +10% +6% 4.8% Average return -3% -6% -5% -10%

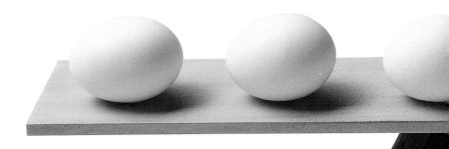

Possible ways to diversify with stocks

By size
To try to mix stability and growth:
- big, stable companies
- mid-sized, established companies
- small, established companies; emerging or start-up companies

By profit potential
Different stocks offer different kinds of profits:
- stocks that pay dividends (regular income)
- stocks expected to rise in price (growth)

By market
To try to capture profits in healthy economies and to minimize losses in unhealthy ones:
- U.S. markets
- European, Asian, and other markets

By industry
Some industries do better than others in certain economic climates.

You **smooth** out the ride

The goal of diversification is to reduce risk: to protect against losing money. But reducing the risk of loss may mean giving up some potential gains. Even if you choose a stellar performer, for example, your overall profits would be reduced by the more modest performances of your other selections. It's a trade-off. You may not make as much as you might have made by "going for broke" with one choice. But you probably won't lose as much as you could have, either.

For example, as the chart on the right shows, someone who invested in both stocks and bonds during the volatile times of 1987 didn't do as well as someone who invested only in stocks, or as badly as someone who invested only in bonds.

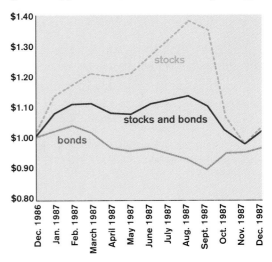

[What happened to $1 invested during 1987]

© Stocks, Bonds, Bills, and Inflation 1995 Yearbook™, Ibbotson Associates, Chicago (annual update work by Roger G. Ibbotson and Rex A. Sinquefield). Used with permission. All rights reserved.

Possible ways to diversify with bonds

By issuer

These are companies and governments who issue bonds to borrow money. The qualities of an issuer affect the level of safety of your investment and whether or not income will be taxable:

- Treasuries (the safest; free from state and local income tax)
- Municipal bonds (free from federal income tax)
- Corporate bonds (taxable)

By quality

To mix goals of safety and maximum income:

- High quality bonds with low interest
- Low quality bonds with high interest

By length of loan

To mix the certainty of short-term loans with the higher income of longer-term loans:

- Long-term bonds (tend to offer higher interest; prices tend to be more volatile)
- Intermediate bonds (the mid-range of interest rates and volatility)
- Short-term bonds (the lowest interest and least amount of volatility)

The markets

To many people, the idea of financial markets seems so complex. It isn't. A market is a market. You go to a supermarket for groceries, a stock market for stocks, and a bond market for bonds. In short, markets

are places where { **stocks and bonds are sold.**

The role **markets** play

Anyone needing to raise money can go to a market to find people looking to invest money. For example, people who want to sell some ownership in their company can go to a stock market where there will be people interested in becoming part-owners. People who want to borrow money can go to a bond market to find potential lenders.

Markets also serve as places where you can instantly see the value other people have placed on an investment. If, for instance, you multiply the price of a share of stock by the total number of shares in the market, you'll get a rough idea what the marketplace thinks the company is worth. (If you bought all the shares, you'd own the whole company.)

The role of **exchanges**

Stock exchanges, like the New York Stock Exchange, American Stock Exchange, and NASDAQ (National Association of Securities Dealers Automated Quotation System), are markets within markets. Their purpose is to help buyers and sellers find each other easily by providing an orderly, open place to trade.

Although each exchange has its own rules (within limits), each provides constant supervision and self-regulation. The quality of that policing affects their credibility—and that tends to filter down to the public's perception of the credibility of the companies whose stocks trade on that exchange.

> **Government supervision**
> The financial markets are tightly regulated. The Securities and Exchange Commission, an agency of the U.S. government, has chief responsibility for protecting investors. They offer a toll-free line to anyone wanting consumer publications or answers to questions. Call (800)-SEC-0330.

{It's an index, not a market}

When you hear that the "market went up or down," you're usually being told about an index, not a market. An index is an indicator of market performance. You can follow several of them every day in virtually any newspaper with a business section.

The most famous index is the Dow Jones Industrial Average. It's a formula created (and sometimes revised) by the editors of *The Wall Street Journal.* "The Dow" tracks the daily gains and losses of 30 stocks considered to be indicative of key aspects of the market and the economy.

The S&P (Standard & Poor's) 500 Index tracks the daily gains and losses of 500 of the largest U.S. companies across a broad range of industries. Many mutual funds compare their stock performance against it.

The Lehman Brothers Aggregate Bond Index tracks the performance of a combination of government bonds, corporate bonds, and mortgage-backed securities. Many mutual funds compare their bond performance against it.

Owning stocks

When you buy shares of stock, you become a part-owner of the company. If the company does well, it may attract more shareholders and cause the price of your stock to rise. If, however, the company doesn't do well, owners like you may decide to sell—which could cause the price to fall. In short, selecting a stock

[means *riding* with the
fortunes of a company.

1 **The management of a small, private company** needs to expand their factory to stay competitive. They could borrow, as they always have, but they have big plans. The only way they'll raise enough money to meet their goals is by sharing ownership in the company with the public and asking people to invest in the company's future.

The company hires an investment banker to "take them public" (offer shares to the public). The banker looks at the company's assets, debts, and profit potential, then calculates how many shares to offer at what opening price. (Not too many shares that they'll flood the market; not too few that they'll be in short supply; not too high-priced that no one will want them; not too low-priced that the company won't raise the amount it needs.)

2 **This is where you come in.** On opening day, the shares enter the market as an Initial Public Offering (IPO). Buyers and sellers negotiate prices on the shares, and at day's end, the management has raised their money. From now on, they share ownership with the public, and the stock will be bought and sold every day on a stock exchange.

Thinking like an owner

Stockholders can earn profits in two ways:

Through distributions of a company's profits, called dividends.

From an increase in the price of a share of the company's stock, called capital gains.

3 Investors follow the progress.
Research professionals analyze the company and distribute reports to the public. Every day, people who want to become owners negotiate prices with people who want to sell their shares. (The company's performance may affect its stock's price, but only by influencing buyers and sellers. The only factors that directly cause a stock price to change are supply and demand: If more people want to buy, the price will go up. If more want to sell, the price will go down.)

4 The company doesn't directly receive more money from the trading.
Still, it benefits from a rising stock price because ownership in the company becomes more valuable and tells the world the company is succeeding.

5 The company's management reinvests its earnings
and continues to do so until they believe they can remain fully competitive *and* share some profits with shareholders. The company begins paying a dividend (distributing profits) for every share owned. By this time, you may have sold your stock and no longer be a shareholder, but trading continues to go around and around as long as the company remains in business.

Owning bonds

By investing in bonds, you're lending money either to a company (buying corporate bonds) or to a government (buying municipal bonds or Treasuries). Either way, it's important to have answers to certain questions: How much should you lend? Is the borrower creditworthy? Will you earn a large enough fee for the loan? When, and how, will you be paid? In other words, investing in bonds

means *riding along* as a lender.

1 **A government agency needs to raise money,** maybe to build, renovate, have operating money, or simply pay off other debts. They hire an investment banker to help.
The banker determines how much money they'll need, how long they'll need to repay the lenders, and the lowest interest rate they could pay and still attract enough lenders (the investors). A bond offering is created, and the government agency is named the "issuer."

2 **They float an offer** (like a trial balloon) to the public to see if they can sell enough bonds at their terms to raise all the money. If they can't, they may either "reprice" and try again or withdraw the offering altogether.

3 **This is where you come in.** You and other people decide to invest. In effect, you say, "I'll lend you this money. I'm willing to earn the interest you're offering and accept your promise to repay my loan plus interest by this set date." For example, you buy several bonds for $1,000 each. They pay a fixed interest rate of 6%, or $60 a year.

> Bonds used to come with coupons you'd tear off and send in to receive your interest. The coupons are gone, but the term remains: Interest rate is sometimes called the coupon rate.

4 **What if interest rates drop?** Your 6% bonds are now more valuable because no one can buy new bonds at 6% anymore.

5 **Some investors decide to sell their bonds; others decide to buy.** Sellers demand a profit (called a "premium") for selling a bond that pays more than the going rate. For example, if the rate is 4%, buyers may agree to pay $1,090 a bond and become the new lenders. They now receive the interest payments and assume the risks of lending.

6 **What if interest rates rise?** Your 6% bonds are now less valuable because investors can do better than 6% by buying new bonds. If the rate is 8%, for example, sellers may be forced to sell at a discount ($919) to entice potential buyers.

7 **Time is up.** The loan ends. Everyone who owns the bonds at this time is paid $1,000 for each one, no matter what their purchase price was.

Thinking like a lender

The amount. Many bonds are initially sold in units of $1,000, called "par value." After that, trading occurs at whatever prices the market will bear.

Issuer. The borrower. Check out the firm's or agency's reputation and the bond's quality rating. This is the best way to gauge your chances of being fully repaid with interest.

Yield. The amount you earn, based on the price you pay for the bond.

Maturity. When the loan is due. You don't have to stay until the end. You can sell the bonds at any time to anyone willing to take your place as the lender.

Call feature. Some bonds let their issuer "call" the bond by a certain date, repay the loan, and stop paying interest. It's a popular feature when rates are dropping because it lets borrowers refinance at lower rates. But it forces you to find other investments—at lower rates.

Mutual funds

If you lack the time, interest, or ability to invest on your own, you can join thousands of others who give their money to a professional money management team. This team pools everyone's money and invests it according to the general goals you and their other clients have agreed to. That's how you participate in a mutual fund. And by joining forces with a large group, you gain access to a different way of investing:

the **power** to do more
than you could do *alone.*

They give you **leverage**

Mutual funds let you use your money like a large investor: There's enough money to diversify among many investments, buy in large quantities (and, therefore, command better prices and much lower fees), and pay for the expertise of professional management.

They'll do more than you would do

Give your money to a pro, and it'll be managed using the tools of a pro. That's what any prospectus will tell you—if you're able to understand the legal jargon.

Many funds are only required to invest 65% of the money in assets that are central to the fund's objective. Managers often use some of the other 35% to:

- push for better returns using options, futures, foreign securities, currencies, and a long list of other sophisticated investments;

- pull back on the risks—using all of the same kinds of investments listed above.

You can also find funds that invest more conservatively and stick to the basics. They may invest 80% or more in the assets central to the objective, even though they aren't required to.

How they **work**

1. You buy shares in a fund generally set up to meet your goal.

2. The price of each share is called the "Net Asset Value" (NAV): the total value of the fund's assets minus liabilities, divided by the total number of shares issued by the fund.

3. After the markets close every day, the new value of the assets is calculated and a new NAV is posted in the papers.

4. Your shares entitle you to any profits, which can come in two ways:

- Funds distribute any income they earn as dividends—even if the fund invests in bonds that earn interest.

- Funds distribute capital gains to shareholder once a year (even though these gains occur any time the manager sells securities from the fund at a profit).

- If you sell shares at a higher price (NAV) than you paid, you'll also earn a profit. Of course, if you sell at a lower price, you'll take a loss.

Prior disclosure { A prospectus tells you how a fund works, what it can and can't invest in, the fees, and other important information. Be sure to read it before investing.

Choose a goal ■ ■ ■

Every fund lists a "fund objective" that corresponds to the three uses of money: either protection, income, or growth (or a combination, such as income and growth, or growth and income, which has the opposite emphasis). This helps you find the right fund for your needs and helps each fund's managers make decisions based on what their clients (people like you) expect of them.

■ ■ ■ then a strategy

Different funds often use different strategies to try to achieve their objectives. Many fund marketing brochures will give you a sense of these strategies. Some managers rely strictly on mathematical models to make decisions. Others make judgments based on a company's products, management, competitiveness, and so on. Here, you may want to select a fund with a strategy that suits your personality.

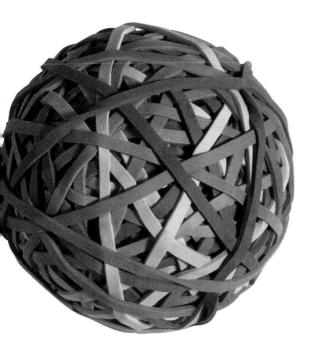

Population explosion

In 1992, there were over 3,500 mutual funds. In 1995, there were approximately 5,700—more than all the stocks on the New York Stock Exchange.

Performance

Every fund tells you: "Past performance is no guarantee of future results." It can't be stressed enough. First, the past doesn't predict the future. Second, there are many ways to compare performance numbers to make a fund look better than it actually is. Choose a fund based on past or current performance at your own risk.

Finding a match for your money

The people who want to use your money usually have specific purposes in mind. They want you to either buy into their business or give them a loan. To try to attract your money, though, they have to create securities, the financial packages you buy as investments. In other words, they try to make themselves appear as attractive as possible to anyone interested in investing. Your task, then, is to

understand the interests

of people who want to use your money.

Small company stocks

These companies need money to expand and grow. That may mean research and development, establishing a product line, or similar uses. Typically, they don't have steady earnings so they reinvest profits back into the company instead of distributing them to shareholders as dividends. People who buy shares in small companies aren't looking for income. They believe the companies will grow and, consequently, make their shares more valuable over time.

Large company stocks

These companies tend to provide more stability by having established product lines and distribution systems. Some have product with consistent, dependable sales even in unfavorable economic climates. Most tend to have enough profits to pay dividends, although amounts are often based on the competitive climate of the company's industry. People who buy these shares of stock often are looking for slow, steady increases in   share prices, with the added benefit of continuous income from dividends.

Personal ads

Young, aggressive stock seeks cash with same qualities for fast-paced relationship. Nothing heavy. Long-term commitment possible but not necessary. Photo please.

Know what you need

The possibilities for using your money may seem overwhelming. But you can handle it. In a typical supermarket there are over 25,000 items, and you're able to shop efficiently. You simply ignore most items and focus only on those you might need. It's the same with selecting an investment: Think of your needs, locate only what might fill them, and ignore the rest.

Short-term bonds

Many companies and governments borrow money for short periods to manage cash flow, cover operating costs, or meet other short-term expenses. They'll pay a small fee (interest) and return your money in anywhere from one day to a couple of years. (The longer they keep it, the more they should pay.)

You can buy individual bonds (corporate bonds, municipal bonds, U.S. Treasuries) or give your money to a bank or mutual fund company to continually do it for you (savings accounts, certificates of deposit, money market funds, and various kinds of short-term, "fixed income" mutual funds).

Long-term

Solid, secure stock wants cash of same for long-term relationship that pays all kinds of dividends. I'm dependable, you're loyal and loving but beyond infatuation. No kids please.

Intermediate and long-term bonds

Corporate and government borrowers also have longer-term needs. For example, companies may need to finance huge projects such as new plants, offices, technologies, or product development. Governments may need to build bridges, hospitals, waste treatment plants, and other community services. The longer they'll have to convince you to part with your money, the more they'll try to entice you with higher interest.

Junk bonds

Some borrowers have difficulty attracting investors (lenders). Money raised from junk bonds often goes to pay off another loan, to pay for a project with a sink-or-swim strategy, or to supply desperately needed operating capital. So these companies have to pay higher interest to balance out your higher risk of losing money.

Wild side

You like to live dangerously for the thrill of high returns. I'm a bond that promises a bumpy ride and lots of payoffs while it lasts. Can we make it all the way to the end together?

[Credit ratings]
Two major companies continually evaluate the creditworthiness of thousands of bonds and distribute their ratings to help the investing public make informed choices. Moody's and Standard & Poor's both use a grading system that goes from triple-A to C or D: The higher the grade, the safer you can consider your money.

Creating a plan

Investing means letting others use your money in return for a fee. It means thinking of money as a tool for achieving some worthwhile goals. A financial plan doesn't have to be perfect. You can always adjust it as you learn. Every goal—and every plan to achieve that goal—

is as **individual** as
the person who makes it.

Where do you want to be?

First, set your goal. Understand what you want to accomplish.

Protection

Do you want to protect what you already have saved? For example, you've saved enough for a down payment on a home. Now it's time to invest in a safe place until you find the right home.

Income

Do you want to earn income? For example, you don't need a lot of money; just enough to be able to take a small vacation without spending what you already have.

Growth

Do you need to accumulate a large amount of money to be able to afford a future event? What, for example, will it cost for your child's college education?

Where are you **now**?

How much money do you have already? How much more will you need?

How much **time** do you have?

When do you have to reach your goal? In terms of investing, it's helpful to think in categories:

- Do you have less than a couple of years?

- Does it feel like you have a comfortable amount—but not a lot—of time?

- Do you need money for an event that is still years away?

[**Another perspective**]

Many financial questionnaires ask you to focus on your "risk tolerance" in a thinly veiled attempt to test your level of investing courage or bravado.

But if you let fear of risk dictate your decisions, you might never make an investment plan at all. After all, everyone has an emotional attachment to money. Maybe it was hard-earned, or a gift, or a family legacy. No one wants to squander it or take unnecessary risks. That's why the first step is to define your goal, and then find ways to use your money as a tool to reach that goal. The goal—and the time you have to reach it—should dictate a strategy. Then you can decide whether the risks in the strategy are worth taking.

How will you get **there?**

ou've gauged how much you'll need. ou've seen how much time you have to ach the goal. Maybe you want to earn a t in a short time. Maybe you want to earn 1 amount that seems appropriate for the nount of time. Or, maybe you're lucky 1ough to have plenty of time to achieve ur goal. Now narrow the field:

/hat investments at least have the potential • achieve your goal? (For the moment, never ind the risks they may pose.)

1 general, stocks are considered well-suited ther for growth or for income. Some stocks e considered relatively stable in price, but 1ere's absolutely no guarantee: Stock prices e unpredictable.

1dividual bonds will earn a predictable 1come within a predictable period. Bond 1utual funds are also geared toward earning eady income but are less predictable.

What could **stop** you?

Now it makes sense to look at the risks. You can assess them in relation to your ability to reach your goal.

Are the risks associated with each potential investment worth taking? If, for example, the risk seems high, are you willing to take it anyway, for fear of not reaching your goal? If not, how far short of your goal are you willing to fall?

Who's Who

Full-service brokerage firms

Despite the advertising, they're much less important than your choice of an individual broker. All the national "Wall Street" firms and many regional firms offer the same benefits. Also, some firms (including some national ones) may tempt their employees to recommend certain investments over others (for the firm's benefit). The most visible difference among firms is what they'll charge you.

Discount brokerage firms

These firms charge lower commissions than full-service firms but only take orders. They don't provide someone who will get to know your needs and help you make decisions.

Mutual fund companies

They offer two main kinds of funds: "Load" funds are sold through brokerages and banks. You pay a sales charge (the "load"). "No-load" funds don't have an up-front sales charge. By saving that charge, you'll have more money to invest. It's often said that "every dollar you invest goes directly to work for you because there are no commissions"; but that's misleading. Most funds charge fees for managing your money, operations, and even marketing (called "12b-1 fees").
These fees are harder to notice since they're deducted from the value of each share you own, not directly from your account.

Banks

They offer investments aimed at protection: savings accounts, CDs, and money market funds. Some offer brokerage services for investing in stocks, bonds, and mutual funds.

Financial advisers

Once called "brokers" and "insurance agents" they usually now call themselves "investment advisers" or "financial representatives." Rather than helping you buy and sell, many want to manage your account and handle all your investing. You'll pay either commissions or a annual fee based on the value of your account. It's most important to find someone you trust no matter which firm he or she works for.

Financial planners

They evaluate your finances and recommend strategies and goals for your overall financial situation. They should be impartial. They're paid a fee for services or commissions on products they sell. Some are salespeople first and planners second. Anyone can be called a financial planner but not a Certified Financial Planner (CFP). These people have passed a rigorous exam run by a regulatory board. They can work either for a firm or independently.

[Appendix]--------→

Following are some of the types of stock investments you'll encounter in the financial world.

"Blue chip" stocks
Stocks of well-known companies with long, established records of success and of paying dividends. Their prices tend to fluctuate less than most stocks, although certain competitive climate can cause them to rise or fall. In general, these are the higher-priced stocks.

"Small cap" stocks
Stocks of companies at the smaller end of the stock scale. "Cap" refers to capitalization, which the price of a share of stock multiplied by the total number of shares you could buy. While these stocks may seem riskier than the stock of larger companies, small caps, as a whole, have actually performed better than any other group over the long term. Over any given short-term period, however, their prices may experience large up and down swings.

Foreign stocks
Stocks of companies based outside the United States. Investors have to deal with all of the variables normally associated with stocks, as well as the effects of currency exchange rates, change in political climates, legal regulations, generally looser regulatory oversight, and a host of other uncontrollable issues.

Growth stocks
Companies with earnings that have risen faster than average. These tend to reinvest their earnings in the business rather than pay dividends, in an effort to remain competitive. Investors believe that, over the long term, the stock will rise in value as the company grows. But the price of these stocks can rise and fall in wider swings than stocks that pay dividends (because they don't attract the investors who would stay invested to earn the income).

Income stocks
Investors don't expect these to gain—or lose—value very much. Instead, they invest for the healthy dividends the stocks pay four times each year. Utilities, such as power companies, are the most commonly held income stocks. While their prices tend to be relatively stable because of the high level of income they produce, they can still suffer drops in price if the competitive climate changes or the market goes through a major decline overall. On the whole, however, income stocks tend not to rise or fall very much, no matter what the overall market is doing.

Cyclical stocks
Stocks of companies whose fortunes are linked with the fortunes of the general economy. If homebuilding is on the rise, for instance, the construction industry will benefit; if building is off the industry will be hurt.

ollowing is a list of the most common kinds of bonds available to
vestors.

S. Treasuries

nese are issued by the federal government and, therefore, are considered the safest of all
onds–because you can always expect the government to repay its debt.

nere are three kinds of Treasuries:

3ills are loans for one year or less.
Minimum purchase is $10,000.
Notes are loans for one to 10 years.
Minimum purchase is $1,000.
3onds are loans for 10 to 30 years.
Minimum purchase is $1,000.

unicipal bonds

sued by state and local governments. You pay no federal income tax on the interest earned,
d no state or local income tax if the bond is issued by the state in which you live. These tend
 pay less interest than taxable bonds, but after taxes, their interest is usually as good or better,
pending on your tax bracket. They're not recommended for tax-advantaged retirement plans
ce those are already tax-free. While your interest payment may remain steady, the price of
e bond may rise and fall with changes in the markets.

orporate bonds

sued by companies that need to borrow money. The interest is taxable; therefore, to induce
vestors, the rates are typically higher than those of municipal bonds. Here, too, your interest
yment may remain steady, but the price of the bond may rise and fall with changes in the
arkets.

igh-yield ("junk") bonds

our chances of not being repaid increase when you invest in these bonds, which carry consid-
able instability and risk because of the financial situations of their issuers. To attract investors,
erefore, companies and governments offer higher interest rates. The price of a junk bond is
ore likely to fluctuate than that of any other type of bond.

ero-coupon bonds

nese bonds sell at discounts from the usual $1,000 each. You don't receive annual interest;
stead, you're repaid the full $1,000 at the end of the term. Still, you're subject to income taxes
 the amount equal to the interest you would have earned each year. You can defer the tax by
tting "zeroes" in qualified tax-deferred retirement plans.

ortgage-backed securities

vestments that earn income from the interest paid by homeowners on their mortgages. If
terest rates drop, the price of most bonds typically goes up. But with mortgage-backed securi-
s, it's different. When rates drop, many people refinance their homes and pay off these exist-
g loans, which gives investors a lower return than originally anticipated.

Following are some of the most common types of mutual funds you ca
expect to encounter, arranged in order here from the most to the least
predictable. Note that the share price of all mutual funds (except, usual
ly, money market funds) will fluctuate and therefore can lead to profits
or losses.

Income earned from a mutual fund is paid as a dividend, even if the
fund receives it from interest paid on bonds it holds. Mutual funds may
also pay capital gains once a year, if securities from the fund have beer
sold at a profit.

Money market funds
Invest in high-quality, short-term securities, often called "cash equivalents" (because they're virtually as good as cash). They seek to keep a stable $1 value per share while earning you steady
but relatively small amounts of income.

Bond funds
Invest in corporate bonds. Income is the goal, and it's taxable. The quality and length of time
until maturity (the end of the loan term) can vary. The price of a share can fluctuate, leading to
profits or losses. So-called "high-yield" bond funds also invest in corporate bonds. Their goal is
to push for higher income, so they often invest in riskier bonds.

Muncipal (or government) bond funds
Invest in municipal bonds or bonds issued by the federal government. You will receive tax-free
income only from municipal bonds issued by your home state. So even if you invest in a fund
focused on your state's bonds, you could owe taxes on income the fund may earn from bonds
issued by other states.

Balanced funds
Invest in both stocks and bonds, seeking a balance of income and growth.

Growth and income funds
Invest in dividend-paying stocks that also have the potential for growth. They usually pay quarterly dividends to fund shareholders.

Growth funds
Invest mainly in stocks, foreign or domestic. The focus is on finding stocks that seem poised for
rises in price. They have higher short-term risk than other funds but have consistently performed well over periods of 10 years and longer.

s a bond investor, will you be lending money to a financially reliable
orrower? Two major firms, Moody's and Standard & Poor's, provide
tandardized, nationally recognized systems to rate the strength of
onds issued by corporations and governments. A bond's rating is con-
nually monitored and revised, keeping the investment world informed
bout its level of creditworthiness.

lany marketing brochures that pitch bond mutual funds refer to these
atings. The list below should give you a better sense of what the rat-
 igs mean. (You'll also find more details on this in the appendix of any
ond mutual fund prospectus).

xplanation	Moody's	Standard & Poor's
onds of highest quality, with greatest likelihood repaying in full with interest.	Aaa	AAA
ery strong; not much difference from highest rating.	Aa	AA
ill reliable but may be susceptible to problems the future.	A	A
ledium-grade bonds; normally adequate, but have pacity to weaken in adverse economic conditions. his is the cutoff point for investment-grade bonds.)	Baa	BBB
onds with few desirable characteristics; Moody's nsiders them to have speculative aspects.	Ba	BB
rimarily speculative bonds; carry great uncertainty id risk in adverse conditions.	B	B
ighly speculative bonds, in poor standing; the lower ted the bond, the more likely it is to be in default.	Caa Ca	CCC CC C C1
onds with the lowest rating, usually in default; ere is little likelihood that investors will be repaid.	C	D

COMPARING TAXABLE AND TAX-FREE INCOME

When you earn interest on an investment, whether it's a savings account, mutual fund, or bond of some kind, the income is either taxable or free from local, state, and/or federal income taxation.

The chart below shows what you would have to earn in taxable income to equal the amount you might earn in tax-free income.

If you earn	it's equivalent to this much taxable income in the following tax brackets:			
	28%	31%	36%	39.6%
3% tax-free	4.17%	4.35%	4.69%	4.97%
4% tax-free	5.56%	5.80%	6.25%	6.62%
5% tax-free	6.94%	7.25%	7.81%	8.28%
6% tax-free	8.33%	8.70%	9.38%	9.93%
7% tax-free	9.72%	10.14%	10.94%	11.59%
8% tax-free	11.11%	11.59%	12.50%	13.50%